MW01204480

What God Really Said

Betty Gannon-Bar

Noble House
Baltimore, Maryland

What God Really Said

Library of Congress
Cataloging-in-Publication Data
ISBN 1-56167-880-5

Library of Congress Card Catalog Number:
2004115958

Published by

8019 Belair Road, Suite 10
Baltimore, Maryland 21236

Manufactured in the United States of America

Preface

❧

Habakkuk 2:3

"And the Lord answered me and said, 'Write the vision and make it plain upon tables, that he may run that readeth it.'

For the vision is yet for an appointed time, but at the end it shall speak and not lie:

Though it tarry, wait for it; because it will surely come, it will not tarry."

This scripture really says:

Describe this dream, this revelation that you contemplate with pleasure.

Declare it, explain it, make it plain on tablet, that he may rush hastily and speedily that comes upon it by chance or by accident or in a hostile manner.

For the revelation and dream that you contemplate with pleasure, is yet for a fixed time and place.

But at the end of the process, it shall kindle a fire and not deceive or be found a lie.

So if it takes time or is delayed, continue to be affectionately desirous of it.

Wait for the time and the season, because certainly and doubtless, it will come and it will not depart.

My Vision. My Call.

My longing and my desire to be used of the Lord became an aching and a burning desire in my heart after I attended a Benny Hinn Partners Conference in Texas in September of 2003.

I met and became friends with a lady who really touched and influenced my heart.

She told me how the Lord was helping her to understand some of the secrets hidden in the scriptures.

When I returned from the conference, I could not get her out of my mind.

I asked the Lord why He would open the word to some and not to others.

This is when the Lord then began to speak to me about surrender. Total surrender.

I thought about Kathryn Kuhlman and how she had given up her own life to do the work of the Lord.

I remembered Benny Hinn telling of how he had asked the Lord to protect and take care of his family as he took up his ministry.

As a very young child, I attended one of Kathryn Kuhlman's meetings and was forever touched by the Holy Spirit.

There is nothing that is more important to me in my life than to allow the Holy Spirit to open the eyes of my understanding, so He can reveal the secrets hidden in The Word of God.

For quite some time my attention became focused on the words in *Ecclesiastes 3:11*. This scripture kept going around and around in my head.

This scripture says, **"He hath set the world in their heart, so that no man can find out the work that God maketh from the beginning to the end."**

Finally the Lord revealed to me that we cannot understand the mysteries in the word, because we have the *world* in our heart.

Our heart is our intellect, our feelings, our mind and our understanding.

I began to fast and earnestly pray. I asked the Lord to take the world out of my heart so I could understand His Word. Slowly but most surely, the Lord began to let me see into His Word.

It is like looking at a layered puzzle, removing the top piece and looking at the one under it, then doing the same with each layer until God Himself, through the Holy Spirit, removed the final one.

This is when the secrets and the mysteries in the Word began to become clear. He began to open the eyes of my understanding.

This was my beginning. My real beginning.

I asked the Lord to let nothing but His work satisfy me. I asked Him to make this work the most important thing in my life.

In His love and patience He began to teach me how to give all things to Him. My children. My job. My finances. My hope.

The Lord told me that if I would trust Him for everything else, He would take care of this.

This, His work, will be read by the atheist, the agnostic and the ones who call themselves Christians, but sadly enough, have never come to know Jesus Christ as their personal savior.

This will be a help to Christians who truly love and serve the Lord. Those who are hungry for fresh bread from the Master's table.

And He wants us to know how very much the He loves us.

This will also open the eyes of those who would like to believe that the devil is a myth.

Just some old, boggy man who frightens little children.

This will explain who Satan was in the beginning and who Satan is now. He is real and he is very much alive.

This will explain why he has such a punishing hatred for man.

The Lord in His loving kindness has revealed to me the simplicity of the Trinity, and He wants to share it with the world.

God wants to give man this beautiful love letter from Him, the Creator, to us, His creation.

In His wondrous love and mercy, He wants to soften man's heart. He wants to open the eyes of this wicked and perverse generation.

The Lord is removing the veil from the eyes of man.

No one will be able to simply dismiss this end time message from God. It will no longer be possible for man to say he did not understand.

There are no titled chapters in this book. The chapters are only numbered. This book will have to be read to see what is next. It is not listed in the table of contents.

This is the Lord's way. Just as this is the Lord's Book.

Chapter 1

The Beginning of the Beginning

Lucifer was the most beautiful and the most gifted angel in Heaven.

Lucifer wanted to sit on the throne. He wanted to rule heaven. He wanted to be like God.

In *Isaiah 14:12-14* Satan believed he could ascend above the heights of the clouds and He would be like the Most High.

He wanted to exalt his throne above the stars of God. He wanted control.

Satan is referred to as Lucifer only once in the entire bible. This was his heavenly name.

When he was cast out of heaven and into the earth, God would not allow him to keep his heavenly name.

He is now recognized by many different names. He is called Satan, the Serpent, the Dragon and the Devil.

These names are really descriptions of who he is and explanations of his character.

Satan means the accuser, adversary and the archenemy of good. His name Serpent means whisperer, enchanter.

To be a whisperer is to slander, to be a talebearer and to oppose Christianity.

The word enchanter means to hiss, to enfeeble. It means effeminacy, to lead astray, and to morally corrupt.

The name devil is used only in the New Testament. Devil means demonic being or supernatural spirit, of a bad nature.

Satan no longer has a heavenly name. He now has only earthly names.

We now have earthly names, but we are promised a heavenly name.

Revelation 2:17 **"To him that over-cometh will I give to eat of the hidden manna, and will give him a white stone, and in the stone a new name written, which no man knoweth saving he that receiveth it."**

The only time Satan's heavenly name is used in the entire bible is when the Lord God Almighty Himself speaks it.

Isaiah 14:12 **"How art thou fallen from heaven, O Lucifer, son of the morning! How art thou cut down to the ground, which didst weaken the nations!"**

No one else had the right or the authority to use that name once God had taken it from Satan.

Isaiah 14:13-14 says, **"For thou has said in thine heart, I will ascend into heaven, I will exalt my throne above the stars of God: I will sit also upon the mount of the congregation, in the sides of the north. I will ascend above the heights of the clouds. I will be like the Most High."**

So, in the beginning Satan knew of God's plan to create man. Satan was already jealous.

Satan already hated man. <u>Before</u> man was created.

We can only imagine how enraged Satan must have been as he watched God create Adam. Out of the dust of the earth. And in His own Image.

Not only had Satan been cast down from heaven, now here he was. This man. And in God's own Image.

Satan watched with rage as Almighty God gave this man authority over all things on the earth.

Satan did not even have enough authority to keep his own name.

Imagine Satan. Hiding in the shadows. Lurking in the darkness. Watching. Listening as The Loving God of creation talked with man.

Chapter 2

Genesis 2:19 says that the Lord God **"brought them to Adam"** all the beast of the earth, all the fowl of the air, every thing that had life, to see what Adam would name them.

"And whatsoever Adam called every living creature, that was the name thereof."

But of all the creatures of the earth there was no help meet found for Adam. No companion. No helper.

Genesis 2:18 **"It is not good that man should be alone: I will make him an help meet for him."**

The Lord caused a deep sleep to fall upon Adam.

Genesis 2:21-22 says, **"He took one of his ribs, and closed up the flesh instead thereof;**

And the rib, which the Lord God had taken from man, made He a woman, and brought her unto the man."

Satan had no idea what man would look like, but Adam was perfect in all his ways, and now, here was this beautiful woman, Eve.

God did not give Satan a beautiful wife, to be bone of his bone and flesh of his flesh.

Satan was never asked to replenish the earth.

God did not give Satan the breath of life. His own Holy Spirit.

The Lord never walked in the Garden, in the cool of the evening with Satan.

Satan's jealousy and hatred for mankind are far beyond anything we are able to imagine.

Satan is filled with a rage that can never be satisfied. Satan's desire and his goal is to murder, to steal and to destroy man.

He wants to keep man out of Heaven, where he himself can never reign. He will be removed from the presence of God, for eternity.

Satan will be cast into Hell that burns with the eternal fire that God Himself has prepared for Satan and those who follow him.

Chapter 3

When the Lord created man He not only designed man's body, but He breathed His own breath into him.

What most people do not know is that the first breath that God breathed into man was the Holy Spirit.

Today we breathe the Breath of Life, but not the Holy Spirit.

John 20:22 says, **"and when He had said this, He breathed on them, and saith unto them, "Receive ye the Holy Ghost."**

His breath. He breathed. <u>The Holy Spirit.</u>

Today we can only receive the Holy Spirit when we are saved through Christ Jesus.

When we are saved, we are washed clean through the precious Blood of Jesus, and only then are we filled with the Holy Spirit. We are then Born Again.

John 3:6-7 says, **"That which is born of the flesh is flesh and that which is born of the Spirit is Spirit. Marvel not that I say unto thee, Ye must be Born again."**

The Lord had given to man of His Holy Spirit.

Matthew 1:20 says, **"Joseph, thou son of David, fear not to take unto thee Mary thy wife: for that which is conceived in her is of the Holy Spirit."**

Luke 1 :35 **"And the power of the Highest shall overshadow thee."**

The word overshadow in Hebrew means breathe.

God took of Himself. Of His breath. The Holy Spirit.

His breath became man's life. Man became a living soul. With a spirit. The Holy Spirit.

God Almighty overshadowed Mary. He breathed on Mary. He took of Himself. He placed of Himself in Mary's womb.

To bring forth the Christ Child. The Son of God. To pay the ransom. To redeem man's soul.

God became man. God lived in man.

God the Father. God the Son. God the Holy Spirit.

The Beauty. The Simplicity. The Plan.

Chapter 4

ॐ

God did not just create man. God designed man. To design is to outline, to plan, to blueprint and to diagram.

To design a building is to create it from the bottom to the top, and from the inside out.

God is able to count the hairs on our head.

Matthew 10:30 says, **"The very hairs of your head are numbered."** *Luke 12:7* says, **"But even the very hairs of your head are all numbered."**

Psalm 139:14 says, **"I am fearfully and wonderfully made."**

This scripture really says:

I am reverently and wonderfully distinguished, made different, and set apart.

Psalm 139:16 says, **"In Thy book all my members were written, which in continuance were fashioned, when as yet there was none of them."**

This scripture really says:

In Thy Book of Record is the written document of the evidence of my structure.

Also of the sequence and succession of my frame which the Potter did write and describe and record.

Which in continuance, and in a great space of time, were fashioned when as yet they were not gathered or assembled. They were not united together.

They were not yet chosen. They were not yet preferred to be a little child that would become a king or a servant or a slave or a maiden.

He has our design, the original blueprint in heaven.

Each fingerprint. Different. Each eye of its own design and color. Every voice with its own sound, its own pattern.

Such planning. So much love. No detail too small or unimportant. All different. Each unique.

Chapter 5

࿇

The Lord was not the father of Adam and Eve. The Lord created Adam and Eve.

The Lord loved the man he had created so much that He wanted to be a father to His creation.

He wanted to protect, to nourish, and he wanted to save man.

In order for God to become the father of man, He had to abide by the laws that He Himself had established for man.

He had to abide by the generational laws of mankind.

The Lord God could not violate or break His own laws. He had to be related to man through a bloodline.

He had to be born into the family of man.

For the Lord to become a father to man, He had to become a man.

The only way He could become a man would be for Him to be born of a woman.

He would have to come through the womb.

Just as Jesus is the only way to the Father, the womb of a woman is the only way for a man to be born on earth.

The Lord took of Himself. He placed of Himself in Mary's womb.

He wrapped His Holiness in the flesh of man so that He could be born of the seed of David.

Chapter 6

❧

Genesis 2:4-5 says, **"These are the generations of the heavens and of the earth when they were created.**

And every plant of the field before it was in the earth, and every herb of the field before it grew."

The Lord even designed the plants and herbs in Heaven before He put them in the earth.

Each plant bearing its own seed. Every leaf, every petal, every flower, beautiful, different.

Nothing in all of God's creation ever was or ever will be the same. No duplicates. No copies.

Nothing by accident. Nothing by chance. All new. All by design. God's design.

Revelation: 4:11 says, **"Thou hast created all things, and for Thy pleasure they are and were created."**

The Lord takes pleasure in all of His creation.

Genesis 1:10-12-18-21 and 25 says, **"And God saw that it was good."**

Good, in the Greek translation, means magnificent, radiant, and gorgeous.

The Lord is very proud of His beautiful creation.

Psalms 53:1 says, **"The fool hath said in his heart, there is no God."**

The word fool means vile, wicked and stupid.

Only a fool can believe there is no God. That all of His beautiful creation was caused by some massive explosion or random chance or, God forbid, evolution.

We can only imagine what that first Adam was really like. He was so intelligent. He had the mind of God. He spoke God's language, the heavenly language.

Genesis 11:4 says, **"Go let us build a tower, whose top may reach unto heaven;**

And let us make a name lest we be scattered abroad upon the face of the whole earth.

And the Lord came down to see the city and the tower which the children of men builded.

And the Lord said, behold, they have all one language; and now nothing will be restrained from them, which they have imagined to do.

Go to, let us go down and confound their language that they may not understand one another's speech."

One language. God's own heavenly language.

This is the same language we speak today when we speak in Tongues. Each of us has our very own prayer and praise language in the Spirit.

Romans 8:16 says, **"The Spirit Itself beareth witness with our spirit, that we are the children of God."**

Romans 8:26-27 says, **"The Spirit also helpeth our infirmities: for we know not what we should pray for as we ought; but the Spirit Itself maketh intercession for us."**

This is how God, Our Heavenly Father, talks with us. Spirit to Spirit.

Chapter 7

Adam and Eve were created sinless. It must have been wonderful to fellowship with God Almighty. The Lord of all creation.

Genesis 2:16-17 says, **"The Lord commanded the man saying; Of every tree of the garden thou mayest eat:**

But of the tree of the knowledge of good and evil, thou shalt not eat of it:

For in that day that thou eatest thereof, thou shalt surely die."

Satan took the words God had spoken to Adam and twisted them. Satan told Eve that they would not die if they ate of the tree, but they would be as God.

Satan beguiled Eve. Satan was just passing time, being friendly. He was misleading her and he was deceiving her.

He was leading her astray. He was cunning and crafty. He told her he was her friend.

He told her he was an associate of God. Lies. The first lies. From the <u>Father</u> of lies.

In *John 8:44* Jesus said, **"Ye are of your father the devil.**

He was a murderer from the beginning, and abode not in the truth, because there is no truth in him.

When he speaketh a lie, he speaketh of his own: For he is a liar, and the Father of it."

After man sinned, he became aware of his nakedness.

He knew no sin until He ate of the tree of the knowledge of good and evil.

After man sinned, the Lord would not allow him to stay in the Garden. This was the punishment for his sin.

When sin was rampant upon the earth and The Lord thought to destroy man, instead in His great mercy and kindness, The Lord saved Noah and his family. The Lord rescued man.

Man will have one final chance of redemption. It will be after the Rapture, during the Tribulation.

He will have to die for the One he was not willing to live for. He will have to be martyred.

Chapter 8

Genesis 1:1 says, **"In the beginning God created the heaven and the earth."**

The word heaven in this scripture is singular. In the Old Testament the word heaven means higher ether, where celestial bodies revolve.

The Word says in the beginning God created heaven, which means there was no heaven in the beginning.

Not until God created it.

God had to create a <u>habitation</u> for Himself, and then He had to create a separate habitation for His creation.

Because there was no heaven. There was <u>God.</u>

Genesis 1:2 says, **"And the earth was without form, and void: and darkness was upon the face of the deep. And the Spirit of God moved upon the face of the waters."**

This scripture really says:

In the beginning, the earth was lying desolate. In waste and ruin. There was destruction, sorrow and wickedness in the surging, greatly agitated waters.

Then the breath of God moved. Brooded and relaxed upon the waters.

Mark 4:39 says, **"And He arose, and rebuked the wind, and said unto the sea, peace be still. And the wind ceased and there was a great calm."**

Jesus was able to calm the storm because the waters had to obey Him <u>before</u>. Before the beginning.

John 1:1-2 says, **"In the beginning was the Word, and the Word was with God, and the Word was God."**

Genesis 1:3 **"God said, Let there be light,"**

Genesis 1:14 **"God said, let there be lights in the firmament of the heaven to give light upon the earth."**

The plural word lights means self-existent, eternal. The word lights is also the national Jewish name for God, which is Jehovah God.

Jehovah God is eternal. Jehovah God is self existent.

Revelation 22:5 says, **"And there shall be no night there; and they need no candle;**

Neither light of the sun; for the Lord God giveth them light."

Genesis 1:16-17 says, **"God made two great lights; the greater light to rule the day, and the lesser light to rule the night:**

And He made the stars also. And God set them in the firmament of the heaven to give light upon the earth."

First the Lord calmed the raging waters. Then He brought forth light, out of the darkness.

Then He divided the waters from the waters and caused there to be dry land. Then God made the sun and the moon and the stars.

God did <u>not</u> create the Universe <u>first</u>.

First He created the earth. After He created the earth, He created the sun, the moon and the stars.

He surrounded the earth with heavenly beauty. He created the Universe to be a help and an adornment for the earth.

Chapter 9

❧

Genesis 1:20 says, **"And God said, Let the waters bring forth abundantly the moving creature that hath life:**

And fowl that may fly above the earth in the open firmament of heaven."

Genesis 2:1 says, **"Thus the heavens and the earth were finished, and all the host of them."**

In Genesis one, there is one heaven. In Genesis two, there are at least two heavens.

Somewhere between the beginning of Creation on the first day and the finish of Creation on the sixth day, the Lord created more than one heaven.

When the Lord said "fowl that may fly above the earth in the open firmament of heaven," there was the only one heaven.

No division between heaven and the earth. Just the open firmament.

God did not say in the sky or in the earth, but in the open firmament, above the earth.

Revelation 4:11 says, **"For thou hast created all things, and for thy pleasure they were and are created."**

The Lord enjoyed seeing His creation flying above the earth in that great expanse. The open firmament of heaven.

At this point in God's time, there was <u>one</u> heaven.

The word heaven has two meanings in the Bible. One meaning in the Old Testament, and a totally different meaning in the New Testament.

The Old Testament heaven means higher ether where celestial bodies revolve.

The New Testament heaven means Abode of God, eternity and power.

Somewhere between the Old and the New Testament, the meaning, if not the very location of heaven, changed.

Chapter 10

࿐

Galatians 3:8 says God **"Preached the Gospel unto Abraham, saying, 'In thee shall all nations be saved.'"**

In this scripture only, the word Gospel means to announce good news in advance, to preach the Gospel.

The Lord preached the Gospel to Abraham, before there was a Gospel. God preached the good news Gospel in advance to Abraham.

In *Luke 16:20* Jesus tells the story of a beggar named Lazarus and a certain rich man. The rich man had everything the world could offer. He lived like a king.

Lazarus would lay at the rich man's gate and he ate of the crumbs that fell from the table. Both men died.

When Lazarus died, Jesus said angels carried him into Heaven. Into the Bosom of Abraham. The rich man died and he was in Hell.

Luke 16:23 says, **"And in hell he lift up his eyes, and being in torments and seeth Abraham afar off and Lazarus in His bosom."**

The rich man begged for a drop of water, but Abraham reminded him of his rich life on earth.

Luke 16:25-26 says, **"But Abraham said, Son, remember that thou in thy lifetime receivedst thy good things, and likewise Lazarus evil things; but now He is comforted and thou art tormented.**

"And besides all this, there is a great gulf fixed: so that they which would pass from hence to you cannot; neither can they pass to us, that would come hence."

The rich man was able to see into heaven. He could <u>not</u> enter into heaven, nor could he leave where he was.

But he could see into heaven. There was no separation or division. There was a gulf.

The word gulf is used only one time in the Bible. In this scripture. Gulf means impassable vacancy.

This is not a parable that Jesus is teaching. People in parables do not have names. These were real people.

They were able to see each other in Heaven and in Hell.

There was only <u>one</u> Heaven.

Chapter 11

Romans 8:21 says, **"For we know that the whole creation groaneth and travaileth in pain together until now."**

This scripture really says:

For we know that the whole creation and all the creatures of the earth experienced a calamity. They murmur and pray inaudibly. In terror and in great pain, running to and fro.

Genesis 6:12 says, **"And God looked upon the earth, and, behold, it was corrupt; for all flesh had corrupted its way upon the earth."**

This scripture really says:

The Lord was aware. He knew that the earth was spoiled and utterly wasted. The Lord knew man had been corrupted and the earth itself had also been corrupted.

Fallen Angels.

Genesis 6:4 says, **"there were giants in the earth and the women of the earth were bearing children to these sons of God."**

These sons of God, the fallen angels that had been cast down from heaven, were now inhabiting the upper ether where the moon and the sun and the other celestial bodies revolve.

Still one heaven. Nothing between. Only the gulf.

The seed that was born of these mighty men and the women of earth were able to live for eternity.

Not only was man wicked and the children of these fallen angels able to live forever, but the earth itself was corrupted.

Chapter 12

The Cleansing

The Lord opened the waters. The fountains of the deep. He had to cleanse the earth of the wickedness and corruption that had been brought upon it by man.

There had never been rain upon the earth, but the Lord told Noah there would be a flood and the flood would destroy all the living creatures on the earth.

The rain would fall and the fountains of the deep would open up. The second heaven was created. After the flood.

Genesis 9:11-17; The Lord made a covenant with Noah.

The Lord set His bow in the cloud as a token of the covenant that He made. The waters would never come again to destroy all flesh.

The word cloud in this verse means: as covering the sky.

Noah and his family stepped out of the Ark into a world that was completely new.

The earth was cleansed from all the sin and wickedness and corruption. And there was a new heaven.

Genesis 6:7 says, **"And the Lord said, I will destroy man whom I have created,"**

Genesis 6:8 says, **"But Noah found grace in the eyes of the Lord."**

This scripture really says:

But Noah found favor, grace and kindness in the sight and countenance of the Lord. The Lord bowed Himself down and was inclined to take pity on man.

The Lord God Almighty, in His mercy, redeemed, recovered and restored man.

Chapter 13

Man's Life Shortened

Man was created to spend eternity protected. In the Garden of Eden.

There was a celestial host of Mighty Angels encamped in the Garden. There was a fenced hedge of protection round about.

Methuselah, who was the oldest man to ever inhabit the earth, lived nine hundred and sixty nine years. Now because of sin, the Lord shortened man's life on earth.

The Lord would now only allow man to live one hundred and twenty years because of his sin and wickedness. This was the second time man's life on earth was shortened.

Man went from living eternally in the Garden of Eden to living just over nine hundred years.

But now, because of his sin, he would only be allowed to live one hundred and twenty years.

Genesis 6:2 says, **"And the Lord said, My Spirit will not always strive with man, for that he is also flesh: yet his days shall be an hundred and twenty years."**

This scripture really says:

The Lord said, My spirit will not always contend with, minister to or plead with man.

He has been deceived and gone astray. Yet in mercy, his days shall be one hundred and twenty years.

Chapter 14

꙰

In all of its beauty, we were only given a glimpse of the full meaning of the 23rd Psalm.

In these end times the Father wants His children to know the fullness of His involvement in our battles and of His great love for us.

The Lord determines where and when the battle will be fought. He determines the rules of engagement.

When we are sorely outnumbered, God Almighty Himself becomes the equalizer.

PSALM 23

"The lord is my shepherd: I shall not want.

He maketh me to lie down in green pastures: He leadeth me beside the still waters.

He restoreth my soul: He leadeth me in the paths of righteousness for his name's sake.

Yea, though I walk through the valley of the shadow of death, I will fear no evil:

For thou art with me; thy rod and thy staff they comfort me.

Thou preparest a table before me in the presence of mine enemies: thou anointest my head with oil; my cup runneth over.

Surely goodness and mercy shall follow me all the days of my life: and I will dwell in the house of the Lord for ever."

This scripture really says:

The Eternal God Jehovah is my friend and companion. I shall not fail or be in lack of anything.

He brings me forth into a beautiful and pleasant place, and He causes me to rest.

He protects and feeds me. He gently guides me. He restores me in this peaceful resting place where I can reverence and adore Him.

He recovers and refreshes my body, my soul, my breath and my appetite.

He protects me and sustains me. He gently guides me on the way.

He cleanses and justifies me. He makes me right again, for His honor and for His purpose.

Yea, though I walk through the narrow gorge of calamity, of pestilence and of ruin;

I will not be put in fear or in dread of any affliction, sorrow, misery or grief.

For thou Almighty God art my companion and my friend.

Thy scepter and thy staff of correction support and protect me.

You console me. You take pity on me. You nourish me and you cherish me.

You spread out a table before me. You announce and you declare the battle in front of my adversary.

You order and set the battle. You join the battle. You are the expert in war.

You are the equalizer in the battle.

You satisfy me with abundance. You accept me.

You anoint me Lord, with perfumed oil.

My lot, my portion, my intellect, my heart and my spirit are wealthy and abundantly satisfied by you, Jehovah God.

Certainly bountiful prosperity, wealth and favor, kindness and mercy shall follow me and pursue me, for as long as I am alive.

I will desire to abide in the family of Jehovah God forever.

Chapter 15

∂

The Lord God remembered the world He created, the way it was before the fall of man.

He wanted the world to have the pureness and the people to have the moral cleanliness and the innocence they had in the beginning.

The only way this could be accomplished was through the Perfect, Holy Lamb of God. His Only Son, Jesus.

JOHN 3:16

"For God so loved the world, that He gave His only begotten Son;

That whosoever believeth in him should not perish, but have everlasting life."

This scripture really says:

For God so loved the world that He wanted to purify and cleanse man. He wanted to justify man.

He offered up His only begotten Son, Jesus.

And because of His wondrous love, however many thousands times thousands of people should entrust their spiritual life and their soul to Him;

And should rely upon Him, should not be destroyed or left behind.

But be in possession of eternal, perpetual rule and to reign and be restored and nourished forever.

Chapter 16

∂⌀

The prophesy of the crucifixion is a twofold prophesy. It tells of what Christ must suffer on the cross. It also clearly tells what He will accomplish.

A new Covenant and Salvation for mankind.

The Prophesy Within the Prophesy

ISAIAH 53

"Who hath believed our report? And to whom is the arm of the Lord revealed?

For he shall grow up before him as a tender plant, and as a root out of a dry ground: he hath no form or comeliness, and when we shall see him, there is no beauty that we should desire him.

He is despised and rejected of men; a man of sorrows, and acquainted with grief:

And we hid as it were our faces from him; he was despised, and we esteemed him not.

Surely he hath borne our griefs, and carried our sorrows: Yet we did esteem him stricken, smitten of God, and afflicted.

But he was wounded for our transgressions, he was bruised for our iniquities:

The chastisement of our peace was upon him; and with his stripes we are healed.

All we like sheep have gone astray; we have turned every one to his own way;

And the Lord hath laid on him the iniquity of us all. He was oppressed and he was afflicted, yet he opened not his mouth:

He is brought as a lamb to the slaughter, and as a sheep before her shearers is dumb, so he openeth not his mouth.

He was taken from prison and from judgement: and who shall declare his generation: for he was cut off out of the land of the living: for the transgression of my people was he stricken.

And he made his grave with the wicked, and with the rich in his death; because he had done no violence, neither was any deceit in his mouth.

Yet it pleased the Lord to bruise him; he hath put him to grief: when thou shalt make his soul an offering for sin, he shall see his seed, he shall prolong his days, and the pleasure of the Lord shall prosper in his hand.

He shall see the travail of his soul, and shall be satisfied: by his knowledge shall my righteous servant justify many; for he shall bear their iniquities.

Therefore will I divide him a portion with the great, and he shall divide the spoil with the strong: because he hath poured out his soul unto death: and he was numbered with the transgressors; and he bare the sin of many, and made intercession for the transgressors."

This scripture really says:

Who hath suffered our hardship or felt our passion and yet trusted, supported and remained faithful to the doctrine?

For He shall ascend, mount up before him as a tender plant and as a root out of a barren desert.

But he will have power and he will rule the nations.

He is brought forth with scorn, as a vile person. But He will endure and bring forth victory,

He is frail and destitute, but He will forbear. He is appointed to establish a covenant.

He is a man. He is Maimed and crippled. He is in anguish, pain and affliction.

He is aware and understands that He is designated for punishment. To be wounded and put to pain.

We hid our faces from him.

He is thought of with scorn, but He will be victorious.

He will endure. He will bare the pain.

We did not think to regard him and we valued him not.

Surly he hath carried away our pain and our sorrows, yet we did plot and contrive for him to be punished, beaten, slain of God. Chastised and afflicted.

He was made sick. He was diseased and grievous with pain for our moral revolt, for our trespass, and for our sin.

He was beaten to pieces and collapsed. He was crushed for our wickedness. For our punishment and for our sins.

The discipline, the correction and the rebuke was for our restitution. For our happiness, our wealth and our prosperity.

It was finished, accomplished and supplied by his steadfast, hour by hour wounds.

And by the Great Physician, we are thoroughly cured, mended and healed. We are made whole.

All like sheep have wandered and gone astray. Every one to his own desire, lust and greed.

All have been ashamed and in disgrace because of the course of their life.

The Lord made him the intercessor and laid on him, the punishment of us all.

He was brought as a lamb to the slaughter and as a sheep to be sacrificed. He was put to silence. He openeth not his mouth.

He was tyrannized by the taskmasters.

He was brought low. He was defiled and ravished. He solemnly stood upright and He opened not his mouth.

He was rapidly seized from the barren prison and from the right to justice.

From the privilege to be judged. From the right to be punished or vindicated by the law.

Who has suffered or experienced his pain or his passion? Who can utter or speak of his fervent, intensely devoted work?

He was snatched away from the Most High God, Jehovah.

They committed sacrilege. He that was Sacred, now was desecrated.

He was robbed. Stripped of his virtue and of his power. Stripped of his strength and of his glory for the trespass, sin and rebellion of My people.

He was wounded and violently stripped.

He made his grave, his sepulcher was with the guilty and the ungodly. With the nobles and with the kings.

In pestilence and in ruin. In Hell.

The Highest God was with him and had charge over him and because he had committed no evil, no injustice or wickedness and because the Honor of the Most High God was to the Son, neither was there any guile or treachery in his mouth.

Yet and still, it was beneficial and advantageous to make him diseased. To oppress him. To humble him and to beat him to pieces.

When Thou shalt make his soul and his breath, a gift and a sacrificial offering for sin, to be punished for sin.

Then He shall see His seed conceive and bring forth, yielding fruit.

He shall lengthen and prolong the days of His seed. They shall rule and reign as Priests.

The delight and pleasure of the Lord shall be pleasant in the power of His open hand.

He shall behold and consider the suffering and sorrow of His soul.

He will be full of satisfaction, by His recognition and understanding of the punishment

My Own lawful righteous justifier shall turn great multitudes. Millions of millions to righteousness and justice.

He shall drive away all of their sin and all of their iniquities. Therefore and rightly so, I will rest content.

And because of His labor and His virtuous work, I will raise up the inheritance. The abundant, exceedingly great increase.

He shall bring out and exalt the prey and the plunder with the powerful and the mighty.

Because He hath poured out, made empty and destitute His soul. Even unto the death.

He was appointed to be made known to those who had broken away in sin and rebellion: He suffered and He bore the blame.

He forgave the offenders. He cleansed and purified millions.

He came between and He interceded for the millions who had abandoned the faith and revolted in sin.

Chapter 17

When Jesus was on the cross He suffered beyond anything we can imagine.

He asks His Father why He has been forsaken.

He reminds the Lord and himself of how the Lord rescued the people of Israel. How they were in fear, and how they were delivered.

He tells the Lord of the shame He is suffering. He also tells His Father He knows why He is there.

He knows His purpose.

He tells His loving Father that He is willing. That He will not fail. That He is still trusting in His faithful loving Jehovah God.

PSALM 22

"My God, my God, why hast Thou forsaken me? Why art Thou so far from helping me, and from the words of my roaring?

0 my God, I cry in the daytime, but Thou hearest not; and in the night season, and am not silent.

But Thou art Holy, 0 Thou that inhabitest the praises of Israel.

Our fathers trusted in thee: They trusted, and thou didst deliver them.

They cried unto thee and they were delivered: They trusted in thee and they were not confounded.

But I am a worm, and no man; A reproach of men, and despised of the people.

All they that see me laugh me to scorn: They shoot out the lip, they shake the head saying,

He trusted on the Lord, that he would deliver him: Let Him deliver him, seeing He delighted in him.

But thou art he that took me out of the womb: Thou dist make me hope when I was upon my mother's breast.

I was cast upon thee from the womb: Thou art my God from my mother's belly.

Be not far from me; Trouble is near; There is none to help.

Many bulls have compassed me: Strong bulls of Bashan have beset me round.

They gaped upon me with their mouths, as a ravening and a roaring lion.

I am poured out like water. All my bones are out of joint: My heart is like wax, it is melted in the mist of my bowels. My strength is dried up like potsherd. My tongue cleaveth to my jaws. Thou has brought me into the dust of death.

Dogs have compassed me: The assembly of the wicked have inclosed me: They pierced my hands and my feet.

I tell all my bones: They look and stare upon me.

They part my garments among them. They cast lots upon my vesture.

Be not thou far from me, 0 Lord: 0 my strength. Haste thee to help me.

Deliver my soul from the sword; my soul from the power of the dog.

Save me from the lion's mouth, for thou hast heard me from the horns of the unicorns.

I will declare thy name unto my brethern: In the mist of the congregation will I praise thee.

Ye that fear the Lord, praise him. All ye the seed of Jacob, glorify him. All ye the seed of Israel.

For he hath not despised nor abhorred the affliction of the afflicted; Neither hath He hid his face from him; but when he cried unto Him, He heard.

My praise shall be of thee in the great congregation: I will pay my vows before them that fear him.

The meek shall eat and be satisfied: They shall praise the Lord that seek him: Your heart shall live for ever.

All the ends of the world shall remember and turn unto the Lord: All the kindred of the nations shall worship before thee.

For the kingdom is the Lord's. He is the governor among the nations.

All they that be fat upon earth shall eat and worship.

All they that go down to the dust shall bow before him: None can keep alive his own soul.

A seed shall serve him; It shall be accounted to the Lord for a generation.

They shall come, and shall declare his righteousness unto a people that shall be born, that he hath done this."

This scripture really says:

My Jehovah God. My blameless, unreproachable God of power. Why hast thou left me destitute?

Why art thou so far removed from me? From my hurt and from my harm.

From defending and rescuing me in my roaring and moaning.

My Jehovah God, I call out in the daytime, but you respond not.

In the night season I am undone and in ambush by murderous design.

Thou Jehovah God, will accomplish, make clean and anoint.

Thou who dwellest in the celebration and singing of praises to Thee, by Thy people.

Our fathers had hope and confidence in thee. And they were secure in Thee. Thou didst cause them to be carried away into safety.

They shrieked from anguish and danger unto you and with smoothness you brought them forth and they did escape.

Their hope, their livelihood and their confidence was in Thee, and they were not ashamed or disappointed.

But I continue and I persevere. I am crimson´and scarlet. I am maimed. I am a mortal man.

I am in reproach. In disgrace and in shame by the hypocrites. Men of low degree.

I am despised and scorned by the congregated people. All they that stare at me, they approve of this and enjoy this.

They have me in derision. They scorn and mock me. They shoot out the lip.

They shake their head saying, He thought there would be justice and that judgement would be carried out.

They say, He trusted on the Lord Jehovah. That the Lord would be willing to cause him to escape.

Surely the Lord was pleased with him?

Thou 0 Quickening Spirit, that caused the fetus to leap in the womb. Thou that took me out of the womb that I would become Peace.

Thou didst cause me to take refuge and to be secure and confident and to trust in Thee when I was yet upon my mother's breasts.

I was brought forth unto Thee from my mother. From her tender loving care.

Thou 0 Quickening Spirit, causing me to leap for joy in my mothers womb, thou art my strength. My Almighty God from my mother's belly.

Be not removed or withdrawn from me. Affliction, distress and tribulation are in place and are ready. There is none to aid or protect me

Abundant and plenteous people of strength besiege me on every side. They prevent me from escaping, to bring me to naught and to defeat me.

The Chief est of Angels fail and are frustrate.

The people violate me. They have trapped me and besieged me. They have crowned me.

They utterly delivered me with their mouths as a ravening and a roaring lion.

I stay in place. I persevere.

My substance and strength are spilled out. My bones are spread and stretched and separated.

My heart is faint with fear and with grief. It melts like wax in the center of my belly.

My might, my power and my substance is shamed. Dried up like potsherd.

My tongue is seized by my jaws.

Thou Jehovah God hast reduced and brought me down to the earth as dust. To the place of the dead.

To fulfill and to accomplish.

Dogs have surrounded and beset me on every side. The assembly of evil doers record, witness, and testify;

They strike me and beat me and stare with eyes wide open:

They, with violence, this day, this hour have pierced my hands and my feet.

I desire, I long to pour out and to recount the price to purchase. To buy, to accomplish and to cause this thing to come to pass.

They approve of it and regard it with pleasure. They pillage and divide my garments. They cast by custom, stones for my clothing.

Publicly and with boldness.

Be not withdrawn or removed. Keep not yourself far from me, 0 Jehovah God, my strong support and protection.

Hurry. Be eager and ready to aid and protect me.

Snatch away my body, my breath and my soul from the evil, from the wicked, and from the sword.

Deliver me, Thy only child. Thy only beloved son, from the exceeding great power of the dog.

Free me. Help me. Deliver me from the lion's mouth.

For You Jehovah God, will respond and will answer me from the comer of the alter, and I will be lifted up.

I will speak and record and celebrate Your honor and Your authority unto my kindred in the midst of the multitude.

I will take pleasure in being your friend and companion. In ruling with You.

Ye that fear and reverence the Lord God Jehovah, boast and celebrate. Sing hymns, ye seed of Jacob.

Honor and promote Him. Reverence Him and stand in awe of Him, all ye seed of Israel.

For He hath not found you vile or contemptible nor filthy or polluted.

Neither hath the Lord concealed or kept His favor and respect from Him.

But when he shouted and cried aloud unto Him, the Lord indeed listened and heard Him.

My song, my celebration and my praise shall be of Thee Jehovah God, in the midst of the great multitude of people.

I will recompense. Make restitution. I will stand boldly and announce.

I will explain to them that reverence and fear Him. The humble, the lowly and the hurt.

Those who are looked down upon and those who are held in low esteem. Those who are dealt harshly with, shall be freely fed with plenty.

They shall dine and rest in quiet; They shall praise and sing and shine unto Jehovah God.

They that diligently seek him and search him out. Those that worship Him.

Your soul, your intellect, and your heart shall be kept alive, nourished and shall be quickened.

For Eternity.

The utter most parts of the earth shall call to remembrance and they shall recognize and come back again to the Lord God Jehovah.

All the tribes of the engrafted Gentile nation shall pay homage. They shall bow down and humbly worship.

In fear and in honor of His countenance. For the Kings realm and rule is the Lord God Jehovah's.

He has dominion and power in the mist of the Engrafted Gentile nation.

And all they that receive and accept him and are anointed upon the earth, they shall feed freely and with plenty.

They shall worship and reverence and pay homage to the Lord Jehovah.

All they that descend down to the enemy, they shall crouch down and they shall bow their knee. They shall fall feeble before Him.

None have the power or the might to revive, to quicken or to keep their own soul.

His seed shall have rule. They shall recount the sum. The price paid by the Sovereign God for the purchase of the remnant.

They shall surly and doubtless come to rule and to reign. They shall boldly announce the perfection, the result and the conclusion of His Virtue.

His cleansing and moral justice unto a flock. A nation of people. A people bewildered and confused in mind. Now brought forth as a beacon.

For He hath done this.

Chapter 18

ॐ

This Psalm gives hope. For safety. For freedom from fear, and for protection from evil. It also speaks of the punishment and judgment of the wicked.

Punishment and Redemption

PSALM 91

"He that dwelleth in the secret place of the most High shall abide under the shadow of the Almighty.

I will say of the Lord, He is my refuge and my fortress: My God; In Him will I trust.

Surely He shall deliver thee from the snare of the fowler, and from the noisome pestilence.

He shall cover thee with His feathers, and under His wings shalt thou trust: His truth shall be thy shield and buckler.

Thou shalt not be afraid for the terror by night; Nor for the pestilence that walketh in darkness; Nor for the destruction that wasteth at noonday.

A thousand shall fall at thy side, and ten thousand at thy hand; But it shall not come nigh thee.

Only with thine eyes shalt thou behold and see the reward of the wicked.

Because thou hast made the Lord, which is my refuge, even the most High, thy habitation;

There shall no evil befall thee, neither shall any plague come nigh thy dwelling.

For He shall give his angles charge over thee, to keep thee in all thy ways.

They shall bear thee up in their hands, lest thou dash thy foot against a stone.

Thou shall tread upon the lion and the adder: the young lion and the dragon shalt thou trample under feet.

Because he hath set his love upon me, therefore will I deliver him: I will set him on high, because he hath known my name.

He shall call upon me, and I will answer him: I will be with him in trouble; I will deliver him, and honour him.

With long life will I satisfy him, and show him my salvation."

This scripture really says:

He that abides in the secret hiding place of protection, in sight of the Supreme Most High God, shall dwell with joy.

In the shade and in the defense of the powerful, unyielding and impregnable Almighty God.

I will declare, I will answer and I will say of The Eternal Jehovah, He is my hope. He is my shelter and my trust.

He is where I flee for protection.

My great and mighty Judge. He holds me. He accompanies me and He enjoys me. In Him will I be confident and secure.

Certainly and doubtless, He will recover me and rescue me.

He will snatch me away from the purpose and the intent of the fowler and from the eagerly, rushing, perverted wickedness.

From calamity and ruin, and from the destroying plague and pestilence.

He shall hedge me round about, He shall protect me and feed me. He shall satisfy me with abundance.

He shall cover thee with His wing. And in His promised Son Christ Jesus, thou shalt rejoice and take refuge.

His faithfulness and His Right Hand shall be the shield of thy protection. Thou shalt be surrounded by thousands of thousands.

Thou shalt not be put in fear of that dreadful thing that walketh in the night.

Nor of the terror in the midnight tempest.

Nor of the thunderbolt from God. The wound and the curse that hides in obscurity.

Nor for the destroying plague that is sent forth. That walks among you in concealment. On a mission.

Nor for the violence that ravishes. Nor for the devastation that wasteth at noonday.

Thousands of thousands shall fall at thy side, and multiplied thousands at thy right hand.

Those that are condemned to punishment, shall die. They shall cease to be. They shall be judged.

But, it shall not be able to attack you or to come upon you and overtake you. It shall not be able to touch you. It shall not come near you.

Only with pardon and the forgiveness of sins will thine eye behold the retribution. The recompense, of the ungodly and of the wicked, of the guilty and of the condemned.

Therefore and because thou hast been determined and committed to make The Eternal Jehovah God, which is my hope and my trust and my confidence, even the Most Supreme High God thy choice, thy retreat and thy habitation;

There shall no calamity or wickedness befall thee. Neither shall any be able to lay a hand upon thee or touch thee in violence. Nor shall any plague come near thy home, thy dwelling place. He shall send His angles with a command to attend thee and to protect thee and to guard thee.

They will be a hedge round about thee. They shall keep thee in the course of life.

They will protect thee along the way.

To lift thee up in their hands and to hold thee, lest thou stumble or stub thy toe against a stone.

Thou shalt tread down and have charge over the fierce lion and the twists and contortions of the adder.

And over the excitement and temptation of the mind, the desire and the reaching out to lust.

And over the hideous serpent, the elongated monster, thou shalt trample under foot.

Therefore and because he hath appointed and set his heart and his desire and love upon Me, I will breathe upon him and refresh him with vitality and carry him away.

I will cause him to escape.

I will set him on high. I will perfect him and I will exalt him, because he hath observed and recognized my position, my character, my Honor, my Authority,

He shall call out to me, and I will breathe upon him. I will accommodate him.

I will pay attention. I will listen and I will respond to him.

I will be with him in distress. I will be with him in tribulation and in adversity.

I will equip him, and I will strengthen him. I will fight for him.

I will make him honorable when he is difficult. I will boast of him when he is an immature Christian. When he is thick and stupid, I will promote him and make him glorious;

With lengthened and fruitful and exceeding great age I will fill him with satisfaction and cause him to experience victory, deliverance, health and prosperity.

Chapter 19

≈

Jesus predication and promise to his disciples fulfilled.

Cloven Tongues

ACTS 2:2-4

"And suddenly there came a sound from heaven as of a rushing mighty wind.

And there appeared unto them cloven tongues like as of fire, and it sat upon each of them.

And they were all filled with the Holy Ghost, and began to speak with other tongues, as the Spirit gave them utterance."

This scripture really says:

And there came a loud roar from eternity, from the Abode of God. The breath of God. A vital, mighty force.

To execute and to accomplish. To verify and to fulfil the prediction of the Son. They saw, with their eyes wide open and they did understand.

They beheld the glowing, fervent warmth of the love that was bestowed upon them.

An allotment, a portion of the benefit for the kindred brother. The mortal man.

To induct him into royalty. To be made ready to reign with the King and to become God's army.

It settled down on the head of each and every man. Immovable and steadfast.

The prediction of the Son was absolutely and fully executed and fulfilled.

The sacred, pure and blameless Holy God, ascended to His throne.

And they began to preach and to cry out. To speak in different and strange languages.

To bring it to pass at the appointed place. To bear fruit, to increase and to grow.

Chapter 20

❧

Jesus wanted to show James and John and Peter His true glory, which was The Glory of His Father.

Jesus Transfigured

In *Matthew 17:2-5* and in *Mark 9:2-7,* Jesus took Peter, James and John up into a high mountain, and in their sight Jesus was transfigured.

MATTHEW 17:2

"And was transfigured before them: and His face did shine as the sun, and His raiment was white as the light.

And behold, there appeared unto them Moses and Elijah talking with Him.

Then answered Peter, and said unto Jesus, Lord, it is good for us to be here:

If Thou wilt, let us make here three tabernacles; one for Thee, and one for Moses and one for Elijah.

While he yet spake, behold a bright cloud overshadowed them: and behold a voice out of the cloud, which said;

This is My beloved Son, in whom I am well pleased; hear ye Him."

This is what they really saw:

And Jesus was metamorphosed. He was changed in figure and in character.

A company, a congregation of people of excellence, which included Abraham, Isaiah and Jacob surrounded Him.

And this was done in the sight of James and John and Peter.

And Jesus face did radiate with the Glory that He labored for; The glory of His lineage, from whom He had descended.

The glory of His Father, Jehovah God.

And His robe and vesture shown as the sun. And behold, with their eyes wide open, they saw something remarkable.

They saw Moses and Elijah talking with Jesus.

They wanted to build a tabernacle. A habitation for Moses, Elijah and Jesus.

But as they were yet speaking, behold, there appeared an illuminated, lustrous cloud. A haze of brilliancy that enveloped the Lord God.

The Lords attendants, the worshipers and the angles and the troops of Nations and also a of people of excellence, were all made manifest.

And a voice spoke out of the cloud and said, "He is the Father of Judgment. He is the Corner Stone who will administer judgment, in whom I am well pleased."

Chapter 21

ॐ

The Perfect Prayer

The most perfect beautiful prayer that we can pray is the Prayer Jesus taught the multitude.

MATTHEW 6:9

"Our Father which art in heaven, Hallowed be Thy name.

Thy kingdom come, Thy will be done in earth, as it is in heaven. Give us this day our daily bread.

And forgive us our debts, as we forgive our debtors.

And lead us not into temptation, but deliver us from evil: For Thine is the kingdom, and the power and the glory, for ever. Amen."

This is what we really pray:

Our blameless, cleansing, sanctifying Most Holy God.

Father of dew.

The I AM that abides in, and makes His habitation heaven.

Thou, that by cutting the flesh and passing between the pieces, makest a covenant;

God of Power.

He that makes His abode in Eternity; give ear when we profess, utter, or call upon Your name.

Thy Kingdom, Thy rule and Thy reign are set in heaven.

Let Thy desire, Thy decree, and Thy Love come into being and be fulfilled and performed in our labor and in our deeds on earth, as it is in Heaven, the foundation of Thy power.

Deliver, divide, and bestow to us our garment, our cover and our veil. Our needful direction.

Give us a gentle, tame day. Bring forth and give us our daily bread. The Bread of Life, Christ Jesus.

Separate, lay aside and omit our faults and our weaknesses as we lay aside and omit the sins of those who transgress against us.

Carry us not into adversity, or piercing trial. Give us comfort in the midst of the resting place.

Bring salvation and victory Deliver us from malice and from corruption. Deliver us from the devil,

For thine is the establishment of Thine Own, and of Thy Covenant,

Thou art the builder and repairer of the Sacred Name of the Lord Jehovah. God of miraculous power.

Thou art tried and approved and honored. To be praised and worshiped in dignity and in glory. Where I will be forever.

Chapter 22

❧

In the book of the Acts of the apostles, what these men of God really witnessed is both beautiful and amazing.

It was not only the Lord ascending into heaven, but the wonderful welcoming committee that came to accompany Him home.

Jesus Ascends

ACTS 1:9

"And when He had spoken these things, while they beheld, He was taken up; and a cloud received Him out of their sight."

This scripture really says:

And when Jesus had spoken theses things, this remnant, this residue of People of Excellence, which included Abraham, Isaac, Jacob, Isaiah and Elijah; All of them received Jesus out of the sight of the disciples.

Chapter 23

࿔

ACTS 1:11

"This same Jesus, which is taken up from you into heaven, shall come in like manner as you have seen Him go into heaven."

The scripture really says:

This same Jesus which was lifted up, with strong support of Mighty Men and was escorted into the glorious, magnificent Abode of God in Eternity;

Shall come back the same way. With strong support of Mighty Men. This remnant, this residue of People of Excellence. They will include Matthew, Mark, Luke, John, Paul and Andrew.

And Jesus will Rapture His Bride out of the sight of the people.

Chapter 24

The Gifts and the Calling

These verses will speak to everyone who has a special gift from God, whether of prophecy or healing or teaching or giving.

Whatever the gift may be, this is what the Lord is saying to His people:

1st TIMOTHY 4:14

"Neglect not the gift that is in thee."

This scripture really says:

Do not be careless or make light of this gratuity. This gift that grants favor and pardons. This gift that rescues and delivers from danger and from passion.

It is a spiritual endowment and a divine influence upon the heart. It is a gift given to you in kindness.

Chapter 25

❧

"Wherefore the rather brethern, give diligence to make your calling and election sure; for if ye do these things, ye shall never fall."

This scripture really says:

"Wherefore the rather brethem, hide and protect this secret thing, this hidden treasure because you are chosen from among them.

Selected and called. For if you do these things you will never err, offend or stumble."

Chapter 26

11 THESS: 1:11

"Wherefore also we pray always for you, that our God would count you worthy of this calling"

This scripture really says:

Wherefore we also pray always for you, that our God would find you suitable, deem you fit and count you worthy.

Chapter 27

This verse gives hope of restoration and guidance in the darkest times.

ISAIAH 43:19

"Behold I will do a new thing; now it shall spring forth; shall ye not know it? I will even make a way in the wilderness, and rivers in the desert."

This scripture really says:

Behold, I will rebuild you, repair you and refresh you. I will answer you. I will commune with you and I will teach you.

I will cause you to bud, to spring up and to grow. Shall you not be aware and have knowledge of it?

I will order and ordain for you, your course in life. I will make a road in the wilderness.

The road will be lightened, even in desolate places.